World Cuisine | **United States**

D1529205

United States

With recipes by:

David Bouley • Jean-Georges Vongerichten

World Cuisine

WORLD CUISINE - United States

Coordination: ESP Promotions Ltd, London
And TP& Associates, Madrid and Milan

For further information on the collection or to purchase
any books that you have missed, please visit:
www.timesonline.co.uk/cookbooks

For further information regarding publication rights,
please contact: cookbookinfo@gmail.com

Original idea
Jaume Fàbregas

Editorial director
Juan Manuel Bellver

Collection coordinator
Núria Egido

Gastronomic Advice
Xavier Agulló
R. de Nola
Jorge Osés Labadie

Editors
Mercè Bolló
Judit Cusidó
Pau Raya Castell
Miguel Ángel Sánchez

Contributing editors
Esther Buira
Lola Hernández
M.ª Dolores Escudero
David Ibáñez
Carles Llurda
Meritxell Piqué
Carles Raventós

Photography
Christian M. Kempin / Gastrophotos
Daniel Loewe / Joan Jolis, S.L.
Miguel Rajmil

Layout
New Color Book, S.L.

Cover Design
WEP Milano

Pre-print
Digitalscreen

Printout
Avenida Gráfica

ISBN 84-609-7351-4 (complete works)
ISBN 84-609-7356-5 (volume IV - United States)
Legal deposit: M-39745-2005

Contents

To whet the appetite

A land of opportunity

When enjoying the cuisine of the United States it is important to look beyond its fast food, its malls, its chains of coffee shops and mile after mile of suburban drive-ins. One must head into the family home or the small town, family run restaurants or to the more upmarket Manhattan bars and restaurants to discover its true essence. Those that are fortunate enough to have the opportunity to visit this vast and diverse country will discover a land that is rich in natural produce both from the sea and from the land. True to the same diversity demonstrated by its peoples, this is a land of adaptation – a real melting pot where old ideas mix with new and where all recipes are not only steeped in history and culture but also moulded to take advantage of the local produce available and in season.

Like so many other countries' cuisines, American cooking says a great deal about its people – how they live and where they come from. Their cuisine mirrors their history: the arrival of the English and the French, the introduction of African slaves, the opening of cultural borders with Mexico and the arrival of the modern day immigrants from Europe and Asia. Their cuisine also reflects the importance of the family and the association of traditional dishes with their national holidays – always a time for family gatherings. However, it is the diversity of their cuisine that sticks out the most and the differences between the four points of this country from the Cajun and Tex-Mex dishes in the southern states to the pies, roasts and chowders in the North. This really is a land of great diversity and the land of opportunity – the opportunity to discover some amazing cooking!

World Cuisine: United States

The film and television industry continues to show a distorted image of American gastronomy, based mainly on the offer of a wide selection of fast food chains with undoubted worldwide popularity. However, the United States also boasts delicious regional cuisine thanks to the direct inheritance and influence from a great variety of cultures such as the European, African, Asian, Mexican and Caribbean cultures.

Yet, is there real gastronomy to be found in the United States, the land of fast food? This is often the typical question posed when studying the culinary customs of the most powerful country in the world. Nevertheless, it only takes a little research to discover that its culinary history has evolved in a similar fashion to many other countries in the world.

The original cooking techniques of the Native Americans has been adapted with the ingredients and cooking techniques brought by the European colonists, resulting in a very rich and varied culinary tradition. However, unlike some countries, the United States has one important distinguishing feature: The United States continues to receive a large and diverse number of immigrants from all cultures that constantly contribute to the continuous evolution of its cuisine. On the other hand, it is undeniable that the media worldwide presents the United States as a 'fast food' culture, dominated by junk food chains. Both the film and television industries promote the average American's eating habits – the trips to the hot dog street stalls, the enormous breakfasts, the family barbeques and their Thanksgiving Day stuffed turkeys. Yet, the roots of even these dishes that make up the stalwart of American cuisine lie in regional recipes influenced by European, Asian, African, Mexican and Caribbean cultures.

The American Cuisine

In most states, the heritage of its local cuisine lies in the arrival of the European colonists that took advantage of the unequalled resources found in the country. Their entry to the United States was mainly through states such as New England, where seafood and fish dishes are predominant, as found for example, in recipes such as *chowder*. These states are also renowned for their dairy products from Vermont, blueberries from Maine and puddings like *pandowdy* and Boston's cream pie. New York also has a great deal of gastronomic diversity, at the heart of which the economic and social importance of the Jewish population is notorious, as demonstrated by the vast number of *delicatessen* stores, *kosher* establishments and the success of *bagels*, the typical New Yorker breakfast. It is also worth mentioning the characteristic *hot dogs* and *pretzels*, both of

with recipes based on rice, like *gumbo*, a spicy soup, and *Hoppin John,* a traditional New Year dish. The state of Louisiana, with New Orleans as its capital city, also has its own culinary style: Cajun cuisine, a curious mixture between Spanish and French cuisine with African and Caribbean flavour. In the southwest, the influence of Mexican cooking is important, although the dishes are not as spicy. Central United States is also the birthplace of the turkey, the chief ingredient in one of the most traditional American feasts, Thanksgiving Day.

The central states are characterised by their lust for meat, and the various

German descent. From the rest of the Atlantic coast states, comes the Brunswick casserole, originated in Virginia and North Carolina; the recipes of the Pennsylvanian farmers, which tend to be all pork related; and the Yankee Pot Roast. Southern cooking is the one that best respects typical ingredients such as corn and beans that were used by the Native Americans. These dishes were subsequently enriched by the British, the French, and the African slaves. In the south east, we find a distinctive type of farm-based cuisine, with many fried foods, thick sauces and desserts. Amongst the favourites are Southern Fried Chicken, corn breads and the much-loved barbeques. The African slaves contributed means of preparation and accompanying side dishes. In the areas closest to the Atlantic Ocean, oven meals are typical as well as the use of sausages. Corn, vegetables and fruits also grow well in this part of the United States and it is here that we find the birthplace of another genuine American dish: *coleslaw*, a cold salad with cabbage and mayonnaise.

With the exception of New York, the real gastronomic laboratories of the United States are the Pacific states, where the influence of the nearby Asian countries and a growing interest in a healthier diet complements the earlier influence of the European colonists. The state of California is the best example of the west coast cuisine, with large fruit and vegetable plantations, and seafood and fish from the cold northern waters. Here, meat yields to creative recipes with fresh ingredients like *Caesar's salad*. California is also a good place to end this brief tour of American cuisine, as it is here that culinary experimentation and daring business projects tend to be born prior to hitting the mainstream worldwide.

World Cuisine

Starters

This collection of traditional dishes
has been created by:

Sergio Omar Pérez
Restaurant Soho

Raúl Pico González
Restaurant Ribs. La casa de las costillas

Matthew Scott
Restaurant Gumbo

Waldorf salad

Serves 4
1 lollo rosso lettuce
1 Romaine lettuce
1 apple
100g nuts
2 celery stalks

For the yogurt dressing:
1 cup yoghurt
1 cup mayonnaise

Wash and cut the lettuce. Peel and chop the apple, chop the peeled nuts and thinly slice the celery. Make a base of lettuce on the plate, top with the mixed apple, nuts and celery and finally pour the well-mixed sauce over the ingredients.

This salad was created in 1896 in the famous Waldorf-Astoria Hotel and was an instant success. Originally, it only had apples, celery and mayonnaise, but then became popular throughout the United States and today every state has its own recipe.

Caesar salad

Serves 4
1 lettuce
50g white bread for croutons
50g bacon
10g grated parmesan cheese
20g tinned anchovies

For the dressing:
250g mayonnaise
5 anchovies
1/2 garlic clove
1 glass of red wine
1 teaspoon Worcestershire sauce
1 teaspoon Dijon mustard

Wash the lettuce, strain, cut in thin strips and put in a salad bowl. Dice the bread and fry using plenty of hot oil until golden brown. Transfer to paper towels and drain excess oil off. Cut the bacon into strips, fry and leave to drain on paper towels. Add the croutons and bacon to the salad bowl, and mix in with the lettuce. Beat together all the ingredients for the Caesar salad dressing and dress the salad. To finish, dust the top with the grated cheese and decorate with the anchovy fillets.

The popular salad is named after César Cardini, a popular Italian restaurateur of the city of Tijuana (Mexico), who created it at the beginning of the 20th century. If you want the dish to be even lower in calories, you can use a salad dressing of olive oil, lemon juice and garlic.

Coleslaw

Serves 4
1/2 white cabbage
1/2 red cabbage
4 carrots
2 medium-sized spring onions
125ml mayonnaise
25ml vinegar
1 teaspoon sugar
1/2 teaspoon celery seed
Salt
Pepper

Wash the cabbage thoroughly and shred. Dice the spring onions and the carrots. Toss the ingredients in a salad bowl. To prepare the dressing, mix the mayonnaise, vinegar, sugar and celery seed together in a bowl. Season with salt and pepper and pour over the salad ingredients. Mix well, place in the fridge for thirty minutes and serve.

Coleslaw can be used as an accompaniment to a great variety of dishes, including fried fish. This refreshing and light salad that comes from Rock Island is especially popular on the fourth of July, American Independence Day.

Level of difficulty: low
Preparation time: 45 minutes
Cooking time: 30 minutes

Potato salad

Serves 4

8 medium-large potatoes
4 hard-boiled eggs
1 spring onion
50ml mayonnaise
100g gherkins
1 tablespoon English mustard
1 celery stalk
Salt
Pepper

Boil the potatoes in their skins for thirty minutes until tender. Drain and leave to cool. Hard-boil the eggs and leave to cool. Meanwhile, dice the gherkins, spring onion and celery. Chop the hard-boiled eggs and cube the potatoes. Mix the ingredients in a dish or salad bowl. To prepare the sauce, mix the mayonnaise and mustard thoroughly, and season with salt and pepper to taste. Pour over the salad and place in the fridge. If desired, spoon some of the sauce into a side dish, so that guests are able to help themselves if they so wish.

Although this recipe for potato salad is the most traditional, an endless number of variations are possible. The potato, a tuber that originated in the Peruvian and Bolivian Andes, combines well with a great number of ingredients.

Level of difficulty: low
Preparation time: 20 minutes
Cooking time: 15 minutes

Fried green tomatoes with remoulade sauce

Serves 4

3 ripe green tomatoes
12 prawns
2 eggs
Flour
A pinch of black pepper
A pinch of cayenne pepper or
paprika
Oregano
Thyme
Salt

For the remoulade sauce:
Juice of 1/4 lemon
1/8 onion
1/2 garlic clove
1 teaspoon mustard
2 teaspoons ketchup
1 teaspoon chopped celery
1 pinch white pepper
1 pinch black pepper

For the remoulade sauce, finely chop the onion, garlic and celery. In a bowl mix the lemon juice, finely chopped onion, garlic, celery, mustard, ketchup and spices. Beat well.

Wash the tomatoes and cut into 3cm thick slices. Season the flour with the spices and then coat the tomato slices in the seasoned flour, dip it in the egg and put to fry in a deep skillet with plenty of hot oil until golden brown. Lay out on paper towels to drain excess oil. Peel the prawns, season with a pinch of salt and cook on a griddle (or lightly fry with a bit of oil). To serve, put three slices of tomato on the plate with three prawns and a bit of remoulade sauce. Serve the rest of the sauce separately in a sauce bowl.

This type of tomato has been extremely popular in the south of the United States since well before fried green tomatoes became famous thanks to the novel by Fannie Flagg, and the film of the same name. It is a traditional American dish, although the remoulade sauce is mainly used in New York.

Level of difficulty: medium
Preparation time: 25 minutes
Cooking time: 20 minutes

Grilled mushrooms

Serves 4

200g mushrooms
1/2 onion
1/2 red pepper
1/2 green pepper
100g ham
150g crabmeat
50g cheddar cheese
1 pinch black pepper
2 teaspoons olive oil

For the béchamel sauce:
20g butter
10g flour
200ml milk
Salt
Pepper
Nutmeg

Warm the oil in a saucepan over medium heat and sauté the chopped onion until softened, for about five minutes. Add the chopped red and green peppers, fry until lightly brown and then add the chopped ham and the crabmeat. In another saucepan or casserole dish, prepare the béchamel sauce. Melt the butter and add the flour. Stir to form a roux and cook for a minute or two before adding the milk a little at a time, stirring vigorously to incorporate it. When you have added all the milk, simmer gently for 5 minutes. When it has thickened, add the first mixture and cook together for a couple of minutes. Clean the mushrooms and only keep the heads, fill them with the mixture, cover with cheese and grill until the cheese melts and is lightly toasted.

This simple recipe is good to serve with any barbecued meat, although it can also be used as a starter. The preparation time can be reduced using the filling leftovers, if any or if you decide to make a larger quantity, to fill another type of vegetable such as courgettes, eggplants, tomatoes...

Level of difficulty: low
Preparation time: 40 minutes
Cooking time: 30 minutes

Candied sweet potatoes

Serves 4
3 potatoes
30g brown sugar
2 teaspoons butter
50 ml orange juice

Wash the potatoes and cook them whole, without peeling, in a casserole dish with water. When tender, drain, let cool and then peel and slice them. Arrange the slices on a baking tray, spray them with the orange juice, sprinkle them with the brown sugar and finally, butter them. Cook in a 180°C oven for about 30 minutes, until the top becomes caramelized.

This dish is usually served on Thanksgiving Day. It is also an excellent side dish for some meat and poultry dishes, especially pork and chicken, which combine beautifully with the sweetened potatoes.

Level of difficulty: medium
Preparation time: 1 hour
45 minutes
Cooking time: 1 hour 15 minutes

Chicken and sausage gumbo

Serves 4
1/2 chicken
1 farmhouse smoked sausage
300g rice
1 onion
2 celery stalks
1 green pepper
2 tomatoes
150g okra
2 bay leaves
1 pinch thyme
1 pinch oregano
1 pinch black pepper
1 pinch cayenne pepper
Plain flour
Oil
Salt

Boil the chicken in a litre of salted water for about forty minutes. When tender, remove, allow to cool, take off the bone and cube. Strain and store the chicken stock.

Peel the tomatoes, chop finely and set aside. Now prepare the *roux*. Place a teaspoon of oil and flour into a saucepan, stir well and continue cooking for about twenty minutes over a very low heat, stirring regularly until well browned. Next, add the finely chopped onion, the celery and the green pepper and cook for about ten minutes, until the vegetables are tender. Add the chopped sausage, the okra and fry lightly for a further five minutes. Next add the pulsed tomatoes and the spices, and stir for a few minutes until the tomato sauce thickens. Finally, add the chicken stock. Serve in deep serving dishes with white rice (for example, boiled and stir-fried in a little oil).

When preparing the *roux*, pay particular attention. Its colour and therefore cooking time depends on the meat that it is accompanying. Okra may be bought tinned from delicatessens or from larger supermarkets.

Level of difficulty: low
Preparation time: 30 minutes
Cooking time: 25 minutes

Fried cheese

Serves 4
2 big mozzarellas
2 eggs
50g parmesan cheese
Pepper
Garlic
Parsley

For the tomato sauce:
2 tomatoes
1 garlic clove
1/2 onion
50g parsley
Salt
Pepper

Cut the *mozzarella* in half and leave aside. Beat the eggs mixing them with the chopped garlic and parsley, salt, pepper and parmesan cheese. Dip the *mozzarella* halves in the egg mixture, coat them with the breadcrumbs and fry in olive oil. Simultaneously, prepare the sauce, sautéing the peeled tomatoes with the remaining ingredients for twenty minutes. Serve the fried cheese on a base of tomato sauce.

Authentic *mozzarella* is traditionally made with buffalo milk and is richer than its cow's milk counterpart.

Level of difficulty: medium
Preparation time: 50 minutes
Cooking time: 40 minutes

Chilli

Serves 4

1 onion
600g minced beef
300g cooked haricot beans
1/2 green pepper
2 garlic cloves
4 ripe tomatoes
15 g tomato purée
Maize or sunflower oil
Salt
Pepper
2 teaspoons chilli powder or:
1 pinch cumin
1 pinch paprika
1 pinch cayenne pepper
1 pinch thyme
1 pinch oregano

Peel the onion and chop finely with the garlic. Wash the tomatoes, peel them and mash them, and finally wash and dice the green pepper. In a saucepan with oil sauté the garlic, the onion and the pepper. When soft, add the meat and fry over medium heat. Add the mashed tomato, beans and tomato purée and the spices (or chilli powder). Leave to cook for about thirty minutes. Season with salt and pepper to taste. Serve hot.

Although recipes with Mexican influence first arrived in Arizona and New Mexico, they are currently very popular and found all over the country. Today, *Chilli* is one of the United States national dishes and the official dish of Texas.

Level of difficulty: medium
Preparation time: 1 hour
20 minutes
Cooking time: 20 minutes

Maryland crab cakes

Serves 4
150g crabmeat
3 slices sliced bread
50 ml milk
1 teaspoon mayonnaise
2 eggs
50g parsley
1 onion
1 teaspoon yeast
Flour
Butter
Oil
Salt
Pepper

For the Soho sauce:
100 ml mayonnaise
50 ml ketchup
20 ml Dijon mustard

Put the crabmeat in a small bowl, cover with the crumbed sliced bread and soak with half a cup of milk. In a large container thoroughly mix in the mayonnaise, eggs, parsley, chopped onion, yeast, a pinch of salt and pepper and add the soaked crab meat. Work the mixture until it becomes a homogenous paste and then split into ten discs and refrigerate for an hour (they can also be shaped like hamburgers). After being allowed to set, heat some teaspoons of butter and oil in a skillet over medium heat, flour the cakes and fry for four minutes or until toasted on both sides. Serve with a well-beaten sauce compiled of mayonnaise, ketchup and Dijon mustard.

These cakes are one of the specialities of the state of Maryland, more specifically Baltimore, where there is even an annual competition. It is recommended to refrigerate the crab paste for at least an hour, ideally overnight, for it to set properly.

Level of difficulty: medium
Preparation time: 30 minutes
Cooking time: 2 hours

Crawfish pies

Serves 4

500g crawfish meat (same as crayfish)
2 tablespoons tomato sauce
1 onion
1/2 green pepper
1 celery stalk
2 spring onions
1 garlic clove
1 teaspoon cayenne pepper
1 egg
Oil
Salt

For the pastry:
25g butter
80g plain flour
1 pinch salt

Melt the butter in a saucepan over a low heat. Add a pinch of salt and the flour little by little until golden, but without allowing it to burn. Stir continuously for thirty minutes until smooth and shape into a ball. Set aside.

Heat a little oil in a pan and add the tomato sauce, the finely chopped pepper, the celery, garlic and the spring onion bulb. Leave to reduce for about one hour. Now add the crawfish meat, the chopped spring onion stalks and the cayenne pepper. Leave to cook for twenty minutes and season with salt. Roll out the pastry and cut into circles. Place the crab mixture in the centre of one of the circles, fold and pinch to seal. Cook in the oven until golden.

This recipe, a New Orleans speciality, takes centre stage during the New Orleans Jazz Festival celebrated each spring, which is attended by numerous jazz and crawfish pie fans.

Level of difficulty: medium
Preparation time: 20 minutes
Cooking time: 20 minutes

Codfish balls

Serves 4
250g cod fillets
2 potatoes
1 egg
1 teaspoon butter
2 tablespoons cream
30g pepper
Vegetable oil
Parsley
Salt

Place the cod into a saucepan of cold water and heat. Just before the water boils, remove the fish and drain. Allow to cool, flake and mash with a fork. Next, mix the fish flakes with the previously boiled potatoes, eggs, butter, cream and pepper. Break off twelve portions of the mixture, shape into balls and fry in plenty of oil.

The boiled potatoes may be replaced by grated parmesan cheese. The combination of flavours gives equally delicious results.

Level of difficulty: medium
Preparation time: 1 hour
Cooking time: 50 minutes

Manhattan clam chowder

Serves 4
600g clams
100g bacon
1/2kg tomatoes
2 potatoes
1 onion
1 stalk of celery
1/4 green pepper
1 carrot
1 teaspoon flour
Salt
Pepper
Tabasco sauce (optional)

Steam the clams in a casserole dish with the lid on so they open, strain them but keep the water. Fry the chopped bacon until crispy in a frying pan without adding oil and set aside. In the same pan, with the bacon fat, fry the onion for five minutes and, when it starts browning add the chopped celery, pepper, carrot and tomatoes. When everything is golden brown, add a teaspoon of flour, stir and sauté for 30 minutes. After this, add the sliced potatoes and leave to cook for about twenty minutes, adding the water from the clams and a bit more water if necessary. Once cooked, season with salt and pepper to taste. Add the clams and optionally, some drops of *Tabasco*.

The traditional clam chowder, originated in New England, is made without tomato, and therefore goes into a thick whitish soup (see New England style clam chowder).

Level of difficulty: medium
Preparation time: 50 minutes
Cooking time: 40 minutes

New England style clam chowder

Serves 4
600g clams
100g bacon
2 potatoes
1 onion
300 ml milk
100 ml cream
2 teaspoons flour
80g grained corn
1 pinch thyme
1 pinch black pepper
Oil
Salt

Open the clams in a casserole dish with the lid on, with water and salt and then leave to drain. Strain and keep the cooking water. Separate the clam meat from the shells. In another casserole dish add some oil, sauté the onions until light brown, add the bacon and fry until crispy. Add the flour and mix well. Then add the clams, milk, cream, thyme, corn grains and diced potatoes. Leave to cook over moderate heat for thirty minutes, season with salt and pepper to taste.

This delicious speciality originated in Boston.

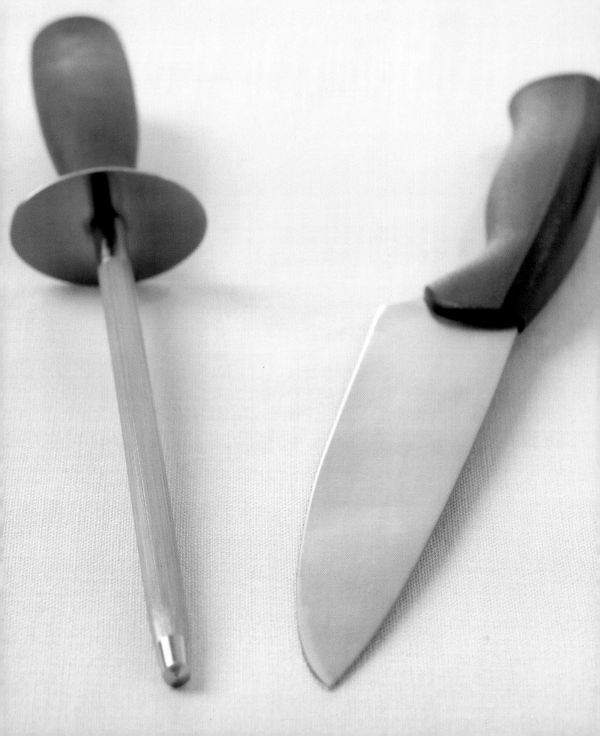

World Cuisine

Main courses

Level of difficulty: medium
Preparation time: 1 hour
Cooking time: 50 minutes

Jambalaya
Rice with meat and langoustines

Serves 4
2 chicken breasts
1 smoked sausage
8 langoustines
300g rice (1 cup per person)
3-4 ripe tomatoes
1 medium-size onion
2 garlic cloves
1/2 green pepper
1/2 celery stalk
1 bay leaf
1 teaspoon thyme
1 pinch salt
1 pinch black pepper
1 pinch cayenne pepper
1 1/2 l game stock (double the quantity of rice)
Salt

Finely chop the garlic, onion, green pepper and celery. Lightly fry in a cooking pot (preferably earthenware) for about ten minutes or until soft and golden. Now add the cubed chicken (previously seasoned with salt) and the sliced smoked sausage. Fry over a medium heat until tender. Remove the meat from the pan. Now add the pulsed tomatoes to the pan and fry lightly for ten minutes. Return the chicken and sausage to the pan, add the spices, herbs, rice, langoustines and the game stock. Stir well and leave to cook over a low heat for about thirty minutes (check the rice to see if cooked). Before serving, season if necessary.

This spicy Creole dish is typical in Louisiana. As well as the basic recipe (onion and garlic *sofrito* with rice and meat or fish), endless varieties of the dish are common: jambalaya with prawns, with turkey etc.

Level of difficulty: medium
Preparation time: 30 minutes
Cooking time: 10 minutes

Soho shrimp

Serves 4

12 langoustines
50g Gouda cheese
50g Cheddar cheese
12 rashers bacon
2 eggs
Breadcrumbs
1 garlic clove
50g parsley

Peel off the langoustine shells and remove the intestinal veins. Split in half and stuff with slices of Gouda and Cheddar cheese. Wrap in a thin rasher of bacon and seal with a cocktail stick. Beat the eggs and add the chopped garlic and parsley. Dip the langoustine into the beaten egg mixture and then coat in breadcrumbs. Fry in oil over a low heat until the bacon is crispy and golden. The dish is often served with Soho sauce (see *Maryland crab cakes*).

This recipe from north San Antonio may also be served with soy sauce. It is preferable to use large langoustines to allow for good presentation.

Level of difficulty: medium
Preparation time: 15 minutes
Cooking time: 40 minutes

Zaccharia skillet

Serves 4
1kg prawns
3 garlic cloves
200g courgettes
200g tomatoes
Parsley
Basil
Salt

Heat a skillet with oil and fry up the chopped garlic and parsley, add the sliced courgettes and the tomatoes and sauté for half an hour over low heat. Season, add the prawns and a bit of fresh basil and leave to cook for about five minutes, until the prawns are exactly right and not overcooked. This dish is usually served with rice and croutons.

This recipe comes from New York. The tomato and courgette sauce is highly coveted and often used as a sauce for pasta.

Level of difficulty: high
Preparation time: 1 hour
Cooking time: 30 minutes

Wrapped sole

Serves 4
4 soles, 200g each
500g Swiss chard
100 ml olive oil
100 ml white wine
1 lemon
Salt
Pepper

Clean the soles and separate the fillets. Arrange in a skillet with the olive oil, sliced lemon, white wine, salt and pepper and cook over low heat for twenty-five minutes. In a saucepan, cook the Swiss chard with water and salt, drain and allow to cool. When the fish is ready, wrap the fillets with the Swiss chard leaves, arrange on a baking tray, brush with olive oil and bake in the oven for five minutes.

This recipe, from Rock Island (Illinois), can also be prepared by wrapping up the uncooked fillets with the lemon and steaming them for fifteen minutes.

Level of difficulty: medium
Preparation time: 20 minutes
Cooking time: 15 minutes

Garlicky bay scallops

Serves 4
500g scallops
3 garlic cloves
1 teaspoon flour
1 medium chilli (optional)
200 ml white wine
1/2 lemon
Olive oil
Breadcrumbs
Parsley
Salt
Pepper

Sear the scallops in a frying pan with oil and set aside. In another pan, fry the chopped peppers and the chilli (optional) with a teaspoon of flour for about one minute; add the seared scallops, salt and pepper and leave to cook for about two minutes. Pour in the white wine and lemon juice, cook for another five minutes and, just before finishing the cooking, sprinkle with a bit of parsley and some breadcrumbs to thicken. Serve with rice.

Scallops are very popular in the United States, although the corals are usually discarded. The most prestigious scallops due to their quality are the ones from Cape Cod bay, which are also much smaller, and the ones from Nantucket Island (Massachusetts).

Level of difficulty: low
Preparation time: 20 minutes
Cooking time: 35 minutes

Grilled codfish in orange sauce

Serves 4
600g cod fillets
200g rice
Oil

For the orange sauce:
Juice of 3 oranges
1 shot of vodka
2 teaspoons corn flour

To make the orange sauce, heat the orange juice and vodka in a casserole dish and reduce to a third of the volume; take off the heat. Let the sauce cool, add two teaspoons of corn flour and mix in thoroughly so it thickens. Boil the rice in water with salt. Meanwhile, cook the cod on a grill over high heat on both sides.

This recipe comes from Rhode Island, where it is said that the Portuguese colonists established the first fishing industry in the United States. Fishing, both industrial and sport, is still one of the principal economic drivers in the area today

Level of difficulty: medium
Preparation time: 1 hour
Cooking time: 40 minutes

Newberg lobsters

Serves 4
4 lobsters
4 mushrooms
3 shallots
2 tablespoons tomato purée
90 ml white wine
150 ml water
15 ml cream
1 tablespoon butter
1 tablespoon flour
30 ml sherry
2 tablespoons oil
1 teaspoon paprika
1 teaspoon salt
Tarragon
Parsley

Boil the lobsters in salty water for seven minutes. Leave to cool and then remove the pincers and empty them. Carefully remove the meat without breaking the shells and set aside. Wash and chop the mushrooms. Take a saucepan and sauté the finely chopped shallots together with the pincers. Add the wine and reduce. Add the tomato purée, paprika, cream, water and salt, blend well and cook over medium heat until the liquid is reduced to a half. Strain using a Chinese strainer and leave aside.

In a saucepan, prepare a roux with the butter and flour, and toast until golden brown. Add the mushrooms and sauté, and then add the previously reserved broth and the sherry. Stir continuously over low heat until it gains the consistency of a béchamel sauce. Sprinkle with some chopped tarragon and parsley. Fill the shells up with the lobster meat cut in large pieces, cover with the roux and grill in the oven to finish.

This recipe can also be prepared with shrimp.

Level of difficulty: medium
Preparation time: 30 minutes
Cooking time: 45 minutes

Tenderloin with lobster sauce

Serve 4
1kg tenderloin steak
Salt
Pepper

For the lobster sauce:
1 lobster tail
2 tomatoes
1 carrot
1 garlic clove
1/2 celery stalk
1/2 onion
1 tablespoon olive oil
30g butter

For the rice:
200g rice
1 onion
2 garlic cloves
50 ml white wine
20g parsley
Oil
Coarse salt
Pepper

To prepare the lobster sauce, put the butter in a pan and sauté the chopped onion, garlic, celery and carrot. When golden brown, add the diced tomatoes and leave to cook for half an hour. Add the lobster meat and cook a bit more. Crush the mixture and leave aside.

To prepare the rice, sauté the onion, garlic and parsley in a pan with some oil. When browned add the rice and stir for three minutes to incorporate the flavour. Add the white wine and, when the alcohol starts evaporating, cover with water and sprinkle with coarse salt and pepper. Leave to cook, drain and reserve.

Once the two side dishes are ready, sear the meat over high heat on each side, salt and pepper and finish cooking on the grill. Serve sliced.

> It is typical in the United States to combine meat and seafood flavours in the same dish.

Level of difficulty: low
Preparation time: 40 minutes
Cooking time: 30 minutes

Baby back ribs

Serves 4

Pork ribcage of 500g
French fries
Salt and pepper

For the barbeque sauce:
1 l Coca-Cola
100g fried tomatoes
50g HP sauce
500 ml beef stock
2 tablespoons soy sauce
1 teaspoon golden syrup

For the coleslaw:
1/4 cabbage and 1/4 red
cabbage
2 carrots
1 onion
125 ml mayonnaise
25 ml vinegar
1 teaspoon sugar
1/2 teaspoon chopped celery
Salt and pepper

For the side sauce:
500g mayonnaise
1 pinch salt and pepper
25g sugar
25g Dijon mustard
3 tablespoons cider vinegar
Juice from 3 oranges

Salt and pepper the ribcage and barbeque, turning every now and then for the meat to cook evenly and brown on both sides. Halfway through cooking, paint the ribs with the barbeque sauce prepared meanwhile, beating up all the ingredients together with a beater. While the ribs finish cooking, prepare the coleslaw (see *Coleslaw* p. 18). Also, prepare the sauce based on mayonnaise beating up all the ingredients. Once the ribs are cooked, remove from the barbeque, paste with this second sauce, cut and serve with the salad and the essential French fries.

This part of the pork's ribcage is named Baby Back Ribs because of its small size, as it comes from the area next to the loin of a young animal. Baby Back Ribs are very tender and juicy, ideal for a barbeque.

Level of difficulty: medium
Preparation time: 1 hour
Cooking time: 30 minutes

Fried chicken with gravy

Serves 4
1kg diced chicken
100g flour
2 eggs
Onion
Paprika
Thyme
Oregano
Sage
Salt

For the gravy:
2 tablespoons oil
2 tablespoons flour
2 tablespoons milk

Clean the chicken thoroughly without removing the skin, dice, salt and set aside. In a bowl, mix the flour together with the finely chopped onion and spices (about half a teaspoon of each one or to taste). Beat the eggs and coat the chicken, covering it well with the flour and then dipping it in the egg mixture. Fry the chicken in a pan with plenty of oil over medium heat: the pieces of chicken should be placed with their skin on the bottom, and turned until very crispy. Drain on paper towels and serve very hot together with the gravy sauce and if wanted, mashed potatoes.

To prepare the gravy, put a couple tablespoons of the same frying oil in into a pan over heat, add the flour and gradually add the milk, constantly stirring until the sauce gains the consistency of a *béchamel* sauce.

Sunday Fried Chicken has been part of the inheritance of southern United States for over a millennium. Even though it seems to be a very simple dish, the controversy over its preparation goes back several generations: whether it should be bathed in milk before serving, whether it should be breaded or not, if it should be cooked with the lid on or not... In any case it must turn out to be extremely crispy.

Level of difficulty: medium
Preparation time: 45 minutes
Cooking time: 35 minutes

BBQ chicken

Serves 4
2 1kg chickens
Salt
Pepper
400g potatoes

For the barbeque sauce:
1l coca cola
100g rich tomato purée or
condensed soup
50g HP sauce
500ml beef stock
2 tablespoons soy sauce
1 tablespoon golden syrup

Split the chickens in two, clean and season generously. Barbeque for twenty minutes. Now leave to soak in the barbeque sauce (see *Baby back ribs*) for three minutes. Remove, lightly shake off the excess liquid and return to the barbeque to finish cooking. Serve with chips.

This recipe is based on the classic dishes that come from Kansas City whose inhabitants are renowned for their love of barbeques.

Level of difficulty: medium
Preparation time: 1 hour
Cooking time: 45 minutes

Cornbread stuffed pork chops

Serves 4

4 thick pork chops
2 slices of cornbread
1/2 onion
1/2 green pepper
1/2 celery stalk
4 bacon rashers
1/2 spring onion, chopped
1 teaspoon cayenne pepper
Oil
Salt

For the cornbread:
1 egg
60g flour
60g cornmeal
40ml milk
2 tablespoons lard
4 teaspoons yeast
2 teaspoons sugar
1 pinch salt

To prepare the cornbread, mix the two flours, yeast and sugar. In another bowl, mix the beaten egg, milk, melted lard and the salt. Next, combine the ingredients and bring together to form a dough. Knead well. Place into a lightly greased and floured bread tin and bake for forty minutes at 150°C. When cooked, remove from the oven and allow to cool before turning out. Set aside.

Split the chops in two down to the bone and open out, seasoning well to taste. Chop the onion, green pepper and celery. Set aside. Cut the bacon into fine strips. Next, fry the onion, pepper, celery and bacon in a dash of oil until soft and golden. Next mix in a bowl with the shredded cornbread and chopped spring onion. Add a pinch of salt and cayenne pepper. Place the mixture between the two halves and sandwich together. Place into an ovenproof dish and bake at 250°C for 35 to 45 minutes. Drizzle with the meat juices just before serving.

It is important that the pork chops are sufficiently thick. The use of spice is optional in this recipe, although without doubt, it adds a special touch to the dish.

Level of difficulty: low
Preparation time: 30 minutes
Cooking time: 45 minutes

Turkey beans

Serves 4
800g turkey
2 spring onions
100g raisins
3 slices white bread, crusts removed
1 green pepper
1 yellow pepper
Juice of 1/2 lemon
2 tablespoons sugar
Salt
Pepper

For the beans:
200g black beans
1/2 yellow pepper
1/2 red pepper
1/2 spring onion
4 bacon rashers
Olive oil

First, prepare the beans. Fry the spring onion and peppers in oil. When golden, add the chopped bacon rashers and then the beans. Mix well and set aside.

Lightly fry the finely chopped spring onions and green and yellow peppers in oil over a very low heat until soft and golden. After about twenty minutes, add the lemon juice, sugar, salt and pepper. Stir well and leave to cook for a further ten minutes. Transfer into an ovenproof dish, place the bread slices over the mixture, and the seasoned diced turkey on top. Bake for ten minutes, remove and stir well and put back in the oven for a further five minutes until the meat is tender and juicy. Serve with beans.

In the United States, turkey is always eaten for Thanksgiving and is cooked as per the recipe above or oven-roasted whole and served with cranberry sauce.

Level of difficulty: high
Preparation time: 20 minutes
Cooking time: 2-3 hours
(depending on the weight of the turkey)

Stuffed turkey

Serves 4
1 turkey
400g hard bread
2 hard-boiled eggs
2 apples
2 onions
2 celery stalks
1/2 teaspoon nutmeg
125g butter
2 tablespoons milk
1 teaspoon dry thyme
1 teaspoon sage
Black pepper
Salt

Clean the turkey and prepare the cavity where the stuffing will go, emptying and cleaning it well. Dice the onions and celery, and sauté over medium heat in a skillet with some butter. Add the bread, previously broken up and soaked in milk, nutmeg and finally the chopped apple and hard-boiled egg. Add spices to taste, sauté the mixture and let cool. Stuff the turkey, putting the mixture into the cavity and then tie up the bird's legs firmly with a piece of string. Baste the turkey with melted butter and put in a preheated 180°C oven for twenty-five to thirty minutes per kilo of turkey (it can take up to three hours, according to the size). While it cooks, it must be bathed with its own juices every now and then and if necessary, a little bit of broth can be added. To see whether it is ready, pinch the legs and if it looks transparent, it is ready. Take out of the oven and leave to rest for twenty minutes covered with a piece of aluminium foil. Serve with its juices and mashed potatoes or with vegetables.

Turkey is closely related to Thanksgiving Day, often being the centrepiece of the feast. The filling must not be too tightly packed, as it needs enough space to swell; if so desired the chest cavity can also be stuffed.

World Cuisine

Desserts

Level of difficulty: medium
Preparation time: 30 minutes
Cooking time: 35 minutes

Brownie

Serves 4
120g chocolate topping
220g butter
4 eggs
220g sugar
70g flour
Nuts
Vanilla ice-cream
50 ml cream (optional)
Butter for greasing

Heat the butter in a bowl set over a saucepan of boiling water and then melt the chocolate (whipped cream can be added at this point if you want the mixture to be creamier). Remove from the heat. Beat the sugar and the flour and gradually add the eggs one at a time until the mixture is completely blended. Pour into a previously greased baking tray, and put in preheated 180°C oven. Cook for about thirty minutes, when the edges of the cake start coming away from the sides of the baking pan, take it out of the oven and decorate with nuts.

The classic brownie, the celebrated *'brownie à la mode'*, is one of the most typical American desserts and is served with vanilla ice cream and topped with melted chocolate.

Cheesecake

Serves 4

600g cream cheese
2 whole eggs
1 egg yolk
1 teaspoon vanilla extract
1 teaspoon sugar
Rind of 1 orange

Mix the cheese, sugar, vanilla, beaten eggs and the grated orange peel in a bowl. Blend in the mixture and pour into a baking pan. Cook in preheated oven at 150°C for 40 minutes. Introduce a tester in the centre to see if it is cooked and it should come out clean and dry. Leave to cool for four hours in the fridge. Serve bathed with strawberry sauce on top or with assorted fruits.

The inhabitants of southern United States' love for all sort of tarts comes from Europe, where the tradition of eating vegetables and fruits cooked in sheets of pastry was originated. In any case, there are recipes of tarts and pies all over the country.

Level of difficulty: low
Preparation time: 30 minutes
Cooking time: 1 hour 50 minutes

New York cheesecake

Serves 4
1 kg cream cheese
200g sugar
6 eggs
2 teaspoons cornflour
25 digestive biscuits
40g butter

Blend the digestive biscuits in a food processor with the melted butter until thoroughly mixed. Cover the base of a flan-ring with the mixture, press down well and bake at 150°C for five minutes. Meanwhile, beat the cream cheese (*Philadelphia*), sugar, eggs and cornflour.

After five minutes, remove the cheesecake base from the oven, cover with the cream cheese mixture, and return to the oven in a bain-marie. Leave to cook for one hour forty-five minutes. Insert a skewer into the cake to test if it is cooked. If it comes out clean, remove from the oven and allow to cool before removing from the mould.

New York cheesecake is perhaps the most famous cheesecake of all, and is often served with slices of fresh fruit, melted jam, chocolate shavings…

Soft scoop ice cream

Serves 4
6 balls vanilla ice cream
6 balls raspberry ice cream
2 ripe bananas
1 tablespoon caramel syrup
1 tablespoon Cointreau
4 chocolate bourbon biscuits
4g chopped almonds

Place all the ingredients (except the biscuits) into a food processor. Blend until creamy. Now chop the biscuits, add to the mixture and continue beating. Decorate the creamy ice cream with chopped almonds.

The texture of this interesting dessert is half way between that of ice cream and milk shake. Flavours may be varied, let your imagination run wild…

Level of difficulty: low
Preparation time: 15 minutes
Cooking time: 10 minutes

Foster bananas

Serves 4

4 bananas
40g butter
50 ml Negrita rum
100g brown sugar
1 teaspoon cinnamon

Peel and cut the bananas lengthwise, into four strips. Dust with brown sugar and sauté in a saucepan with the melted butter. When golden brown, pour in the rum and flambé. Serve them by putting four slices of banana on each plate, pour some rum on top and sprinkle with cinnamon. They can also be served with a scoop of vanilla ice cream.

This is a famous pudding from southern North American cooking, that was created in Brennan's restaurant in New Orleans to take advantage of the bananas that came into the city's port from Central and South America. At Brennan's over a thousand kilos of bananas are flambéed a year.

Level of difficulty: medium
Preparation time: 30 minutes
Cooking time: 1 hour

Lemon cake

Serves 4

1 sheet of puff pastry
125 ml liquid cream
125g sugar
60 ml lemon juice
25g corn flour
2 egg yolks
Water

For the meringue:
5 egg whites
300g sugar

Line a cake mould with the puff pastry and cook in a 200°C oven for ten minutes. Meanwhile, heat up the sugar covered with water in a saucepan and bring to a boil. In a bowl, mix the lemon juice with the corn flour and egg yolks, and then add to the dissolved sugar (adding more water if necessary), until it becomes a homogenous creamy mixture. Pour onto the pastry and cook in the oven for about forty-five minutes.

Prepare the meringue. Beat the egg whites until stiff. Add 4 tablespoons sugar and continue beating until white and glossy. Fold in the remaining sugar with a spatula a few spoons at a time. Cover the cake with the meringue and grill in the oven at 250°C for four minutes.

The cake is served warm and freshly grilled. The secret of the recipe is in the choice of the lemons… if possible they should be of a very juicy variety with a delicate flavour.

Level of difficulty: medium
Preparation time: 1 hour
40 minutes
Cooking time: 1 hour 20 minutes

Pumpkin pie

Serves 4
1 medium pumpkin
2 eggs
1 egg yolk
40g brown sugar
30g white sugar
1/2 teaspoon cinnamon
1/4 teaspoon Nutmeg
50 ml milk
50 ml cream
Whipped cream

For the short crust pastry:
180g flour
40g lard
40g butter
4-5 tablespoons water

For the pastry, mix the flour, butter, lard and water in a bowl and leave to stand.

Put the pumpkin in a 250°C oven for approximately forty minutes. When cooked, leave to cool. When it is cool enough to be handled, peel and mix with the cinnamon, Nutmeg, eggs, milk and cream. Work the filling together and pour onto the pastry, which should have been previously rolled and laid out in a cake mould. Cook for forty minutes. Decorate with the whipped cream to taste.

This is a typical Thanksgiving Day pie. In the south of the United States, it is made with potatoes, but in the north, it is made with pumpkins.

Level of difficulty: medium
Preparation time: 40 minutes
Cooking time: 25 minutes

Apple bread pudding

Serves 4
1 apple
30g raisins
2 eggs
1/2 l milk
75g sugar
1 loaf of hard bread
1 teaspoon cinnamon

For the caramel sauce:
4 teaspoons sugar
1 tablespoon cream
60 ml Bourbon

First, soak the raisins in the Bourbon and leave to marinate for a long time. Then, beat up the eggs in a bowl; add the milk, sugar, raisins and the cinnamon. Put the bread into the mixture until it absorbs all the flavours and goes moist, for twenty to thirty minutes. Knead the resulting dough for a minute or two and put into individual cake moulds. Bake in a 200°C oven for about twenty minutes.

To make the caramel sauce put the sugar and cream into a saucepan and warm over medium heat, constantly stirring until reaching a caramel consistency; add the Bourbon and leave to boil for five minutes. Finally take the pies out of the oven, remove from the cake moulds and pour the sauce on top and cover with slices of apple.

In summer, apples are often replaced with peaches.

Authors' selection

David Bouley
Bouley Restaurant
(New York)

Born in Storrs (Connecticut),
Bouley studied in France under
great chefs such as Roger Vergé
and Joel Robuchon. Back in the
United States, he became
successful with restaurants such
as Le Cirque and Montrachet.
In 1987 he opened Bouley, which
received huge accolades from
the Gault Millau guide and the
Zagat Survey. Having closed
down his restaurant in 1996 in
order to focus on new projects,
Bouley reopened it in 2002 with
huge success.

Jean-Georges Vongerichten
Jean Georges Restaurant
(New York)

Born in Strasbourg (France) and
trained by prestigious cooks like
Haeberlin, Bocuse and Outhier,
Vongerichten arrived in Boston
in 1985 to open the Lafayette
Restaurant. Renowned as
a founder of prestigious
establishments, he currently
holds 10 stars from The New
York Times split amongst his
restaurants JoJo (3), Vong (3)
and Jean Georges (4). Inspired
by French and Thai cooking, he
is considered one of the greatest
chefs of American cuisine.

David Bouley | *Quark soufflé*

Serves 4
1 cup quark cheese
6 tablespoons sugar
3 eggs (whites and yolks separated)
1 teaspoon of vanilla extract
Grated rind of 1 lemon
A pinch of grated orange rind
Butter to grease the ramekins

Put half the *quark* cheese in a strainer covered with a piece of cloth, and leave to drain overnight in the fridge so that it loses any excess water. Preheat the oven to 190°C and grease six ramekins with butter and then dust with sugar. Beat the egg yolks in a large bowl and add the drained refrigerated *quark*. Then add the rest of the *quark*, the vanilla and the lemon and orange rind and mix. In another bowl, beat the egg whites until stiff, adding the six tablespoons of sugar gradually and then slowly blend into the *quark* mixture. Divide the mixture between the six ramekins, and put each one into individual Pyrex bowls of about 20-25 centimetres in diameter, filled with boiling water in order to cook them in Bain Marie. Bake in the oven for sixteen minutes, until fluffy and golden brown. Serve directly in the ramekins or remove from ramekins very carefully.

David Bouley | *Yellowtail tuna*

Serves 4
For the spinach base:
3 tablespoons butter
3 diced shallots
1 teaspoon salt
2 chopped garlic cloves
100ml cream
1 stalk of fresh thyme
150ml vegetable broth
350g smooth leaved spinach, clean, without stalks
Freshly ground white pepper
Cayenne pepper
Freshly grated nutmeg

For the yellowtail tuna:
350g yellowtail tuna fillets, cut horizontally in 8 equal slices
1l vegetable oil
8 garlic cloves without peeling
1 twig fresh thyme
1 leaf fresh laurel
Fine salt
Freshly ground white pepper

Spinach base: Stir the butter in a wide saucepan with high sides over medium heat, until the lacteous solids fall to the bottom of the saucepan and acquire a toasted nutty colour. Sauté the shallots until softened, add the garlic so it browns, add the cream and thyme and leave until it has reduced to a third. Add the vegetable broth, and when it comes to the boil add the spinach and cook over low heat. Remove the thyme and with the help of a skimmer put the spinach and shallots into a blender, and make a purée. Season with half a teaspoon of salt, white pepper, a pinch of cayenne pepper and nutmeg to taste. If necessary, add a bit of the cooking liquid for the purée to have the desired liquid consistency.

Yellowtail tuna: Heat a large high-sided skillet with plenty oil (halfway full); add garlic cloves, thyme and laurel leaf and heat to 65°C. Put the fish on the herbs, in such a way that the slices are not on top of each other and that they are submerged but not touching the bottom. Fry the fish for 8 to 10 minutes at a constant temperature of 65°C. When it is cooked halfway through, set aside on a plate with paper towels and season with salt and pepper.

Continued on next page

For the caviar and vodka sauce
1/2 cup sour cream
2 tablespoons vodka
2 1/2 teaspoons chopped shallot
1 teaspoon orange rind
1 teaspoon fresh herbs (chervil,
parsley, tarragon and chives)
Lemon juice
Sea salt
Freshly ground white pepper
2 teaspoons Osetra caviar and a
bit more to decorate

For the potato:
1/2 potato
Freshly minced chives

Caviar and vodka sauce: Boil the sour cream in a casserole dish over medium heat. After coming to a boil, leave for four minutes so it is reduced to a half, lower the heat and add the vodka, shallot, orange rind, herbs, lemon juice and salt and pepper to taste. Keep hot and just before serving add two teaspoons of caviar.

Potatoes: Chop the potato on a board with a knife until the pieces are the size of small croutons. Heat a pan over medium heat and lightly brown adding the chopped chives at the end.

Presentation: Put a tablespoon of spinach purée on each plate to make a round base. Arrange two lines of potatoes on the spinach purée and put two tuna fillets on each plate. Pour the caviar sauce on top of the fish and decorate with caviar and parsley.

David Bouley

Gently heated salmon with apple and rosemary purée, Estiria Wurzelgemüse and radish sauce

Serves 4

For the apple and rosemary purée:
3 Granny Smith apples, peeled, without seeds and cut in fine slices
1/2 stick of cinnamon
1 clove
1 glass of white wine
1 tablespoon of butter
1 stalk of rosemary

For the Estiria Wurzelgemüse:
3 cups vegetable broth
1 carrot, peeled and cut in strips
1 white beetroot peeled and cut in strips
1 cabbage turnip peeled and cut in strips
1 turnip peeled and cut in strips
1 small courgette peeled and cut in strips

For the salmon:
8 salmon fillets, without their skin of 100g each
2 tablespoons butter
1 tablespoon butter
3/4 cup onion oil
1 tablespoon lemon juice
1 10 cm radish
Salt
Freshly ground black pepper

Apple and rosemary purée: Wrap the cinnamon stick and the clove in a piece of cloth. Tie the packet up with a piece of string and put into a large casserole dish with the apples, wine and sugar. Put the lid on and cook for ten minutes, then take the lid off and leave for half an hour, stirring every now and then until the water from the apples has evaporated. While the apples are cooking, melt the butter in a saucepan over medium heat, for about five minutes until it browns, then add the rosemary and stir until a layer of foam appears on the top. Remove from the heat and leave to stand and infuse for at least five minutes. Once the apples are cooked, remove the herbs and mash into a smooth purée.

The *Wurzelgemüse*: Bring the vegetable broth to a boil in a casserole dish and then blanch all the vegetables separately (approximately two minutes for the carrots and beetroot, a minute and a half for the cabbage turnip, a minute for the turnip and twenty seconds for the courgette).

The salmon: Preheat the oven to 120°C and salt and pepper the salmon fillets. Grease a baking tray with butter and put the fillets with some nut-sized pieces of butter on top. Cover the tray with foil and put in the oven for ten minutes.

Continued on next page

Presentation: While the salmon is in the oven, heat the *Wurzelgemüse* in a casserole dish with a tablespoon of butter for about four minutes. Put a tablespoon of apple purée as a base on each plate. Place the salmon fillets on top with two tablespoons of *Wurzelgemüse*. Pour the onion oil mixed with a pinch of salt and the lemon juice around the salmon and top with a bit of grated fresh radish.

David Bouley

Passion fruit-banana toffee with espresso chips and meringue

Serves 4

For the passion fruit cream:
100g passion fruit purée
1/2 leaf kaffir lime
Half a chilli pepper
Rind of half a lime
4 sheets of gelatine
3 eggs
100g sugar

For the banana toffee:
500ml milk
100g cream
1/2 vanilla pod
50g sugar
125g bananas
36g caramel

For the coffee chips:
1,250ml espresso coffee
25g sugar
1/3 gelatine sheet

For the meringue:
125g egg yolks
40g sugar
0,5g citric acid

Passion fruit cream: Bring all the ingredients to the boil and when they come to the boil, remove from heat and leave to stand for a day. Sieve and put to boil again, adding four sheets of gelatine, remove from heat and set aside. Beat the eggs and mix with the sugar in a *Thermomix* at 85 °C, until obtaining a thick cream, and then refrigerate and store.

Banana toffee: Bring the milk, half the cream and the bananas to the boil. Meanwhile mix the sugar with the caramel and gradually add the remaining cream. Boil the bananas until they are soft, and then slice and add to the caramel mixture. Beat all the ingredients up until obtaining a homogenous cream and, just before serving, beat again.

Coffee chips: Mix all the ingredients and refrigerate, stirring every now and then.

Meringue: Mix all the ingredients, sieve and pour into a siphon with it. Once it is full, shake and let stand for five minutes before serving.

Presentation: In a shot glass, arrange the different mixtures in layers. First the passion fruit cream, the banana toffee on top, then the coffee chips and finally the meringue. Caramelise the meringue with a blowtorch if possible.

Jean-Georges Vongerichten

Roasted rack of lamb, cardamom crumbs, broad bean purée

Serves 4
1 lamb ribcage
Butter
Garlic
Mint

For the crumbs:
60g breadcrumbs
50g butter
2 teaspoons cardamom (crushed)
1 teaspoon salt

For the broad bean purée:
350g cooked broad beans
1 teaspoon extra virgin olive oil
1 teaspoon water
1 teaspoon salt

Lamb ribs: Slice the ribcage into two, each piece of approximately 150g, and peel the ends of the bones. Tie the meat around the lower part of the bone, giving it a round shape and bake in the oven with oil. When it is almost ready, baste with a paste made of butter, crushed garlic and mint to taste.

Cardamom crumbs: Melt the butter in a saucepan, add a pinch of salt and fry the breadcrumbs and cardamoms until they are crispy and brown.

Broad bean purée: Mash all the ingredients until obtaining a smooth purée, pour into a bowl and cool in a container with ice or in the fridge.

Presentation: Leave the lamb to stand and, just before serving it, baste the upward side again. Serve arranging the broad bean purée on the bottom, the lamb ribs on top and cover with the crumbs.

Jean-Georges Vongerichten

Char-grilled foie gras wonton, red papaya, passion fruit and spiced red wine

Serves 4
For the *foie gras*:
1 foie gras
Wonton pasta sheets
Salt
White pepper
Red papaya
Watercress
Maldon salt

For the lime gelatine:
225g lime zest
85g sugar
1 teaspoon salt
2 teaspoons corn flour
2 tablespoons water

For the passion fruit syrup:
1kg sieved passion fruit pulp
2 green Thailand chillies,
washed and minced

The *foie gras*: Cut the *foie gras* into rectangles, season with salt and white pepper and leave in the freezer for thirty minutes. When it is semi frozen, put in the middle of a griddle or a very hot frying pan and sear on each side, without allowing it to cook. Then, put into a container and refrigerate immediately for about thirty minutes so it solidifies. Once solid, cut into one centimetre sheets and mount the *wonton*: put the pasta sheets on a table, baste them with an egg yolk, put a piece of *foie gras* on each one and fold in half. Cut the ends of the pasta on each side in order to obtain four by two centimetre rectangles.

Lime gelatine: Dissolve the corn flour in water and beat with the lime zest and the rest of the ingredients. Put the mixture into a saucepan and bring to a boil slowly stirring. Add the remaining lime zest, strain using a Chinese strainer and set aside in the fridge.

Passion fruit syrup: Heat a saucepan, combine all the ingredients and leave to reduce until a syrup forms. Strain using a Chinese strainer and store in the fridge.

Continued on next page

For the red wine syrup:
1,5l red wine
1l port
115g sugar
60g cinnamon in sticks, split and toasted
30g toasted and ground allspice
20g toasted and ground pepper grains
20g toasted and ground star anise
15g toasted and ground cloves

For the *panko*:
Fresh white breadcrumbs
Olive oil
Salt

Red wine syrup: Mix all the ingredients in a saucepan; bring to a boil and leave to reduce until a red wine syrup forms. Then strain using a Chinese strainer and set aside.

Panko: Pour some olive oil into a frying pan and when very hot fry the breadcrumbs until golden brown. Generously sprinkle with salt and leave at room temperature on a piece of paper towel. (*Panko* breadcrumbs are coarse and crisp breadcrumbs available in Asian supermarkets. You can use fresh white breadcrumbs instead.)

Presentation: Peel the papaya and cut the pulp into two and a half centimetre side diamonds. Put five diamonds of papaya in a bowl and brush with lime gelatine. Generously pour the passion fruit syrup around the papaya and then the wine syrup, using a proportion of two measures of passion fruit syrup per one of wine syrup. Cook the *wonton* in boiling water and add to the dish. Sprinkle with the panko and decorate with watercress.

Jean-Georges Vongerichten

Chocolate and peanut cake with bitter chocolate sorbet and salty praline

Serves 8

For the cake:
400g egg whites
450g sugar
100g hazelnut flour
100g peanut flour
50g wheat flour
2 tablespoons chopped hazelnuts and peanuts

For the chocolate and peanut ganache:
750ml cream (35% fat)
500g milk chocolate
385g peanut butter
Sea salt

For the chocolate and peanut praline:
100g white chocolate
240g fondant
250g peanut butter
250g hazelnut praline (50%)

For the chocolate and caramel mousse:
600ml whipped cream (35% fat)
120g egg yolks
80g sugar
1g sea salt
160g hot cream (35% fat)
290g chocolate topping (61%)

The cake: Beat the egg whites gradually adding sugar. Sieve the three flours and mix in. Sprinkle the chopped hazelnuts and peanuts in a cake tin and add the cake mixture, then bake the cake in a 350°C oven until toasted. Turn out immediately after removing from the oven.

The ganache: Bring the cream and salt to the boil, and when boiling add the peanut butter. Mix everything together. Pour over the chopped chocolate in three stages, to form three layers.

Chocolate and peanut praline: Melt the chocolate, beat the peanut butter and the praline together, and add to the melted chocolate and then add the *Royaltine*. Spread on a sheet of greaseproof paper, cover with another sheet and roll into a fine roll that should be kept in the fridge.

Chocolate and caramel mousse: Prepare a dark caramel sauce with sugar and salt and mix in some hot cream. Bring to a boil and gradually add the beaten egg yolks. Remove from the heat and stir until cool. Melt the chocolate topping to 50°C and add a bit of cream until an emulsified topping forms. Add the remaining cream, mix and pour into a tray.

Continued on next page

For the chocolate foam:
150g milk chocolate
150g cocoa butter

For the peanut caramel:
2 tablespoons honey
85g butter
5 chopped toasted peanuts
5 chopped toasted hazelnuts
2g sea salt
250ml cream (35% fat)
Milk

For the chocolate sorbet:
1l water
285g sugar
60g icing sugar
150g cocoa powder
225g good quality chocolate (64%)
2g salt

Chocolate foam: Melt the chocolate with the milk and melt the cocoa butter separately and, once melted, mix together. Keep warm.

Peanut caramel: Caramelise the honey with the salt, add the butter and mix in. Add the cream, constantly stirring, add the nuts and, if necessary, add milk until reaching a caramel texture.

Chocolate sorbet: Put the water, sugar and the icing sugar in a saucepan to boil. When the mixture starts boiling, add the cocoa powder, stir and add a bit of salt. Next, add the previously chopped chocolate and emulsify.

Presentation: Put a layer of chocolate pie on a tray. Cover with the *ganache* and leave to set in the fridge. Remove the praline from the freezer, remove one of the sheets of paper and place the praline on top of the *ganache*. Using a bit of pressure, then remove the other sheet of paper.

Finally add a layer of mousse and keep the pie in the freezer overnight. Turn out the pie, cover with the chocolate foam and return to the freezer for an hour. Then, cut each one of the portions, place one on each plate and decorate the slice with *pan d'oro*, some caramelised salted peanuts around it and a small scoop of chocolate peanut topping and a scoop of chocolate sorbet. A small stick of chocolate will make a nice final touch.

Wines

In spite of the limited viticulture knowledge of most Americans and the restraint set by the Prohibition Law in the 1920's, the United States has become a world force in wine production in only the last two centuries. The country's principal wine growing regions are situated along both coasts.

As they extended their presence across the United States, the European colonists began to discover different natural areas, in which they tried to develop a new wine industry. However, these first attempts were full of set backs, for example, the presence of *phyloxera*, the low quality of the native grapes and, later on, the effects of the Civil War. Amongst the more notable results were those of the Jesuit and Franciscan missionaries who planted the first vineyards in the West North American coast, from today's Mexico up to California. The object of these first plantations, mainly run by fray Juniper Serra in the last decades of the 17th century, was to have enough wine for Holy Communion. The variety of grape planted by the monks was called *mission*, today known as *criolla*. Since then, the US wine industry has struggled with many obstacles that have restrained its development, primarily driven by the ignorance of the populations' knowledge of fine wines, limiting the consumption of high quality wine to a restricted market. Another factor that prevented quicker development was the famous Prohibition Law that banned alcoholic drinks between 1919 and 1933. During that period, the few wineries that did exist were able to survive thanks to the production of wine for Holy Communion and grape juice. Once this law had been abolished, the American wine industry started to grow and began its great expansion during the last decades of the 20th century. Today, vineyards can be found in almost every state of the country, even though the main wine areas are in the states of California and the northeast of the Atlantic coast.

California

The state of California currently produces almost 90% of American wine, thanks to its exceptional climatic conditions. However, this region did not exploit its unequalled resources until the late 1960's, when the number of wineries began to multiply, and at this time, the quality of the wines produced also started to increase. California's wineries, unfettered by traditional European ways, have always relied heavily on the use of the technology and research, with a view to finding the best varieties to be used in each area. Currently, the map of Californian vineyards along the state goes from the central Napa valley, behind the coastal range, to the coastal regions. The diversity of its wineries and the scarcity of regulations, allow one to find all sorts of different wines, with a strong traditional predominance of white wines and an increasing interest for red wines. The most common varieties among white wines are Chardonnay, Colombard, French or Chenin Blanc. Amongst the reds Sauvignon, Merlot and Syrah are the most popular. Most notable of all is native Zifandel, a very sweet and versatile grape that allows the production of light rosé wines to complex reds.

Of the varying viticulture regions in the state of California, the Napa and Sonoma valleys are its most distinguished. In the former, the Napa river forms a narrow valley between volcanic mountain ranges, with a landscape that has up to three different climates, as well as many sub-areas. Among the most recognised wines of the Napa valley are the dry white Chardonnay wines, the red Cabernet Sauvignon wines with a lot of body and the famous red Zinfandel.

To the west of Napa is the valley of Sonoma, wider and flatter, where some of the best wines are produced for blending. Most of the wineries in the Napa and Sonoma valley have attractive villas; open to the public and offering free wine tasting at very reasonable prices. This close association with the consumer is to be found across most of the other regions: Mendocino, where the production of mild red wines is predominant; Carneros, an area currently under development, with a dominance of the Chardonnay variety; Santa Cruz and Monterrey, the land of white wines; or Santa Barbara, whose wines appear in the successful movie *Sideways*.

California is also the region of choice for many European companies that have entered

the American market. Among the most prominent examples, we find the Catalan cavas, with Freixenet leading the way. The commercial ability of this firm has allowed it to become the greatest sparkling wine producer in the world. Along the Pacific coast, there has also been an important development of vineyards, especially in the northern states like Washington or Oregon that have climatic conditions very similar to those of the European wine regions.

The Eastern States

Despite California's supremacy as the countries' centre of viticulture, we must also note the increasingly important role of the Eastern states, such as New York, Pennsylvania, Ohio and Virginia. Amongst them, Virginia is the one that continues to follow most closely traditional viticulture, following in the footsteps of President Thomas Jefferson who started the production of good quality wines at the beginning of the 19th century.

Today, the wineries of the area still take advantage of the institutional support that they were granted, and continue to produce wines that very often surprise the specialists. Most of the vineyards are concentrated in the area known as Monticello, in honour of the manor house that belonged to Jefferson himself. In the north, next to the border with Canada, some vineyards are scattered along the coast of Lake Ontario that abates the extreme climatic conditions and allows the production of remarkable Chardonnays and Rieslings.

Lastly, it is worth noting the initiative to introduce a wine industry along the Hudson River and in Long Island. These regions are taking advantage of their closeness to New York in order to secure a solid market.

Index